disc

Plants and the Environment

by Jennifer Boothroyd

first step nonfiction

Lerner Publications Company · Minneapolis

Plants need the **environment.**

Plants use land and water.

3

Plants get food and water
from the **soil.**

Their roots grow in the soil.

The roots soak up water
and **nutrients.**

Plants use animals
and other plants.

7

Animals drop seeds. New
plants grow from these seeds.

Insects carry **pollen** from plant to plant.

9

Some plants grow on trees.

Many plants grow in the shade of taller plants.

Plants **adapt** to their environment.

A cactus holds water
in its big trunk.

Some trees lose their
leaves in the fall.

Some plants have large
leaves to get more sunlight.

Thorns protect some plants
from being eaten by animals.

Plants use the environment
in many ways.

Earth's Shrinking Forests

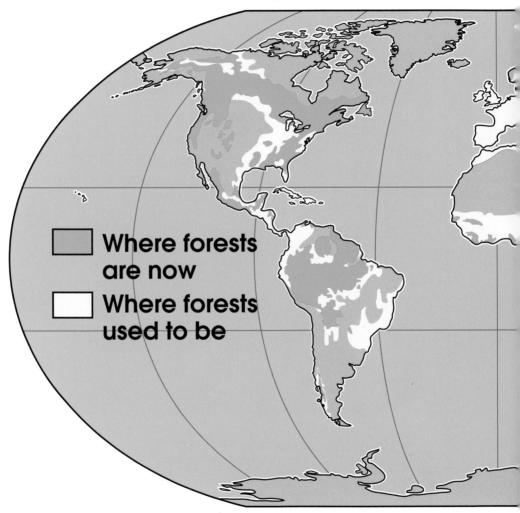

Where forests are now

Where forests used to be

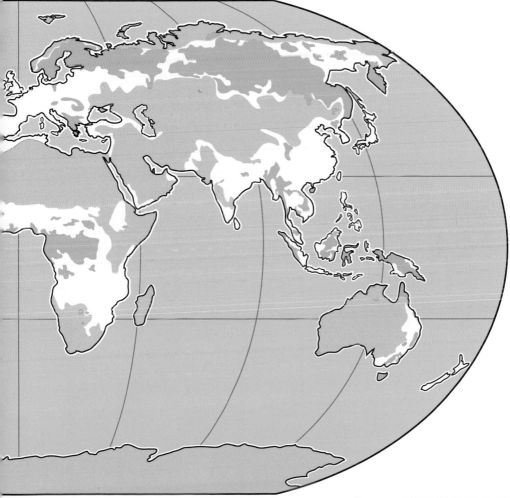

Shrinking Forests

The world's forests are getting smaller. Sometimes nature causes forests to shrink. Storms can knock down trees. Usually people cause forests to shrink. We cut down trees for wood and paper. We clear forestland to make farms and neighborhoods. Luckily, people are changing how they treat forests. We recycle paper, so fewer trees need to be cut down. Companies that cut down trees plant new ones. These changes can stop the forests from shrinking.

We Need Forests

- Wood is used for fuel, paper, furniture, and homes.

- Trees help make oxygen. Oxygen is a gas in the air. All animals need oxygen to breathe.

- Millions of plants and animals live in forests.

- Roots hold soil in place so the rain doesn't wash it away.

- People enjoy camping and hiking in forests.

Glossary

 adapt – change

 environment – the land, water, air, weather, and living things of the earth

 nutrients – elements in soil that plants need to grow and live

 pollen – yellow dust in a plant used to make seeds

 soil – the top part of the ground

Index

The images in this book are used with the permission of: PhotoDisc Royalty Free by Getty Images, pp. 2, 3, 5, 6, 8, 9, 11, 13, 17, 22 (second from top, middle, second from bottom); © Royalty-Free/CORBIS, pp. 4, 22 (bottom); © Richard Eastwood/CORBIS, p. 7; © Vanessa Berberian/Stone+ /Getty Images, p. 10; © Steve & Ann Toon/Robert Harding World Imagery/Getty Images, pp. 12, 22 (top); © Laura Ciapponi/Photonica/Getty Images, p. 14; © James Balog/Aurora/Getty Images, p. 15; © Stephen St John/National Geographic/Getty Images, p. 16; © Laura Westlund/Independent Picture Service, pp. 18-19.

Front cover: © Taylor S. Kennedy/National Geographic/Getty Images

Lerner Publications Company
A division of Lerner Publishing Group, Inc.
241 First Avenue North
Minneapolis, MN 55401 U.S.A.

Website address: www.lernerbooks.com

Library of Congress Cataloging-in-Publication Data

Boothroyd, Jennifer, 1972-
    Plants and the environment / by Jennifer Boothroyd.
        p.   cm. — (First step nonfiction. Ecology)
    Includes index.
    ISBN 978-0-8225-8603-6 (lib. bdg. : alk. paper)
    1. Plant ecophysiology—Juvenile literature. 2. Plant ecology—Juvenile literature.
    I. Title.
    QK717.B66 2008
    581.7—dc22   2007007810

Manufactured in the United States of America
1 2 3 4 5 6 – DP – 13 12 11 10 09 08